A
TENTED
PEACE

BY KATHLEEN McPHILEMY

Fat Dad (Camden Institute 1983)
Dulse and Yellow Man (Hearing Eye 1988)
Witness to Magic (Hearing Eye 1990)
Virtual Reality (Hearing Eye 1993)

A TENTED PEACE

Kathleen McPhilemy

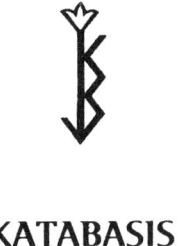

KATABASIS

First published in 1995 by KATABASIS
10 St Martins Close, London NW1 0HR (0171 485 3830)
Copyright: Kathleen McPhilemy 1995
Printed by SRP, Exeter (01296 29271)
Cover painting by Anna Mieke Lumsden

Trade Distribution: Password Books
23 New Mount Street
Manchester M4 4DE (0161 953 4009)

ISBN: 0 904872 24 6

British Library Cataloguing in Publication Data:
A catalogue record for this book is available
from the British Library.

KATABASIS is grateful for the support
of the London Arts Board.

ACKNOWLEDGEMENTS

'House Mouse' appeared in *Acumen*
'Accounts' appeared in *Oxford Poetry*
'Interned' appeared in *Verse*
'The Pall-Bearers' appeared in *Fortnight*
'Hard News' appeared in *The Rialto*

CONTENTS

Blackthorn	1
Japonica et cetera	2
Hard News	4
Accounts	7
Avoiding the Cracks	8
The Deceiver	9
Elsinore	10
The Pall-Bearers	12
Complicity	12
Pheasants and Bombers	14
Deserted Garden	15
Back to Eden	16
Fruit and Veg	17
Bad Breath	18
Exile	19
Trouble Breathing	20
Christmas 1989	22
Good Friday	23
Thorpe Park, Easter 1991	24
Interned	26
The Integrity of Our Quarrel	27
Castlederg	28
Place Names	30
Manners of Speaking	33
Night	34
Towards Rathlin	35
Cloud	36
At Home	38
House Mouse	39

Only Words	40
Let there be Commerce Between Us	41
Loft Door Banging	42
The One and Only	43
New Growth	44
Transmissions	45
Feel Good	46
Visit to the Farm Museum	47
Remembrance Service at Wheatley Park	48
Grace	49
Redemption Song	50

BLACKTHORN

Who has seen the blackthorn
gift of the lengthening evenings?
Pledging another spring
it mantles the edge of the wood
and white as the ghost of March
flowers by the edge of the road.

Whose is the blackthorn blossom?
Does it belong to the name at Lloyds
who owns these woods and fields?
Where among the shivering walls
that have built the cardboard city
could the blackthorn blossom flower?

The flower itself is a wall
hiding that shameful city;
its fires of invisible anguish
are a white and burning bush.

JAPONICA ET CETERA

Again the valentine tree
erupts into blossom;
its fleshy kisses lip along the wall
abashing the delicate
and chastely blushing
Japanese plum.

So much easier to linger underground
blind and safe and warm.

Yet daffodils
coy as shepherdesses
crook their necks
to the enormity of rain
that batters them to life.
Their golden trumpets flare
in a soundless salutation
brief, and pointlessly brave.

Crocuses falter through the earth
brighter than snowdrops
more vulnerable
kicked aside by dogs and children
while polyanthus flowers
sturdy, cheerful, vulgar
turn faces up like plates
to greet us.

Light returns to the afternoon
and milky green prickles on our branches.
Fragile buds, defying frost to come
attend on spring, that old recidivist
who threatens us with hope.

HARD NEWS

1

I'll be glad when all this over, you said
and we can get back to normal. But all this
is never over and there's no such thing as normal.
Normal was the picturebook I lived in
my primary-coloured, taken-for-granted childhood.
Normal was the pistol-hipped policeman
conducting traffic, smiling as I passed.
Perhaps some people grow up all at once
for me it isn't finished and happens slowly.
You would say it's foolish to look harder
that speaking out's a risk that's uninsured
and honesty's no guarantee of truth.

2

The coot's chicks, fuzzy at the edges
pursue their parents, August evening fishing
take from their beaks unchecked the tinsel minnows.
This you'll not dispute, which I have seen
as Shelley might have, or Hopkins walking here.
It's hard to imagine Shelley looking down
and Hopkins wouldn't countenance the blur
where nettles blow in a surround of unnamed green.
After so long I've found the fretty chervil
realised cow parsley lanes of childhood
and Queen Anne's Lace from school all come together
to fringe the paths I really daily use.

3

Paper words, pictures in the paper
someone has taken, the mother's staring eye
the starving baby with his old man's head
going beyond her, unmaking her by dying.
Does he feel pain, that photographer
when you deny his picture; and the journalists
with only their flakjackets between them and the war
when you deny the stories of the camps
do they feel anger, or pass to the next assignment?
Your broader picture shrinks us all to worms
denies all heroes, the dogged trudging boy
leading his family towards a feeding station.

4

I walk my dog where nothing's written down
just grass and rain, where wind lays lines on water.
But without the bridge of words, transmitted signals
the screen translates to pictures on its weft
how shall I reach beyond my range of eyesight?
Camera crews with reporters are dispatched
to search out bits of truth and send them back.
You'd laugh if I said they were errant knights
and I'm an ironist in waking hours
I don't believe in heroes. But heroes always
were faulty, vain, good-living. They were human
projected large to give us pride and size.

5

Too personal, you say, too heart-on-sleeve
the persona on those strings, why isn't she dancing
to the tune of fiddles in a bombed-out square?
I'll show you windows where the glass is gone
Rapunzel knows it and still she combs her hair.
Four gamblers deal outside the main hotel
a wounded dog is screaming by the fountain
while shells come in that no-one hears or dares.
These are metaphors, I remind you
borrowed from another zone of war;
we have our own, and from it messengers
come up behind us, tap us on the shoulder.

6

All this, you would say, is just a story:
the partial versions, the genuine mistakes
even the lies, all roll the action forward.
Why not just accept things, you would say
let the normal curtain drop back down
across the open window, let things blur
leave fishing in the slippery wealth of words
for sharp as silver stabs of correspondence.
I answer: this is a tented peace, we owe
to those who live beyond, a true account
of what we have and know, and to their messengers
entertainment, and our informed attention.

ACCOUNTS

I could escape all this
in a whirling abstraction of violet
or obfuscation of inherited lace
scented with camphor and damp

that usurps a history of polishing
as mahogany discolours and swells
and a mortal rigour of photographs
is abandoned on yellowing walls.

I could forget all this
to wander in imaginary houses
with the rustle of a rich-woven meaning
just ahead through a closing door.

There, in those windowless rooms
where death is a tone or a flavour
and we dance in the late afternoon
to the tune of a refined synaesthesia

I could escape and forget
the improper and vulgar fractions
that blur under my watering eye
and won't add up.

AVOIDING THE CRACKS

I was walking along the path through the meadow
grass on one side, grass on the other
and the river at a distance

thinking desultorily of this and that
when I saw I was taking big steps and little steps
trying to avoid the cracks in the concrete.

Embarrassed, I put my foot down firmly
across a gaping fissure; then, whoosh! no warning
away went everything: my fine feather bed

my sturdy red bricks, the phone on the wall
the kitchen calendar, concepts of teatime
slipped through the gap like money through my fingers.

I wouldn't have minded going on that way
grass on one side, grass on the other
and the river at a distance

if it weren't for the children who appeared beside me
pulling at my hand, their mouths getting wider
threatening to drown me in their noisy darkness.

THE DECEIVER

The stone by the fireplace suddenly
has the face of a fox or a cat;
shapes are changing and fragments
jar the blades of the garden;
you can't see the cat for the trees
or the cage is the bars of his coat.

Path through the woods in sunlight
snares, and the man has a gun;
with a flick of his tail he deceives us
disassembled in the shift of a shadow
the rustle of birds in the bush
an empty pattern of leaves.

The man who has sat at our table
has an alternate look in his eye
is fluent in more than one language
but can be still as the ghost of a cat;
you may see him in a sideways glance
but the mirror won't see him at all.

ELSINORE

Our feet were always wet
guarding the gates.
Our hands prickled at the braziers
glowing and smoking
but there was no real heat.
Inside, neither;
hectic all right, with huge fires
and a fuel store of piled-up logs
dragged in from surrounding villages;
those grates were empty
ghosts of disaffection swirled around them
and the freezing fog.

That was the coldest, wettest year
slush and mud;
the women never noticed us
twitching past in their long robes;
their hems were always draggled
their faces flamed with drink
the air was stale with perfume
nothing was clean.

So when he came
with his close-cropped soldiers
it seemed like good sense
it seemed like the spring.
We didn't resist.

Everything's better now:
nearly everyone has nearly enough
the might-have-been king
is our cultural heritage
and it never snows at Christmas.

THE PALL-BEARERS

Four women in black with beautiful faces
shoulder the coffin that holds their brother
the second they've buried. Perfectly choreographed
with faultless timing they reach the grave.

Who can touch them now or remember
their little fat legs in wrinkled knee-socks?
Who can imagine them now in the office
drinking coffee out of plastic cups?

They have wrapped themselves in the sound of the sea
as it breaks all winter on barren coasts;
they ghost by night through the roads of the hinterland
fourfold rendering of an ancient mirage.

Did you know what you did when your dropped your poison
as they sat on your knee or drowsed before sleep?
Did you count the cost in lovers and brothers
as you reared them up to the art of sorrow?

COMPLICITY

'You have beautiful hands,' she said.
'Hands that control, fingers for music.
I imagine your hands on a push-button phone
fingers for buttons, fingers for bombs.
Visit me with your beautiful hands.'

'You have beautiful hands,' she said.
'I imagine your hands in leather gauntlets
with metal studs, on the rein of a horse
on a bike's handlebar, on the wheel of a car.
Visit me with your roving hands.'

'You have beautiful hands,' she said
'not cacked and chapped, not grained with dirt.
I imagine your strong executive fingers
signing orders, confirming decisions.
Visit me with your managing hands.'

'You have beautiful hands,' she said.
'My eyes are entranced by their delicate strength
the dancing lines of sinew and vein.
I imagine your fingers among the counters of war.
Will you visit me now with your gentle hands.'

PHEASANTS AND BOMBERS

Immense, slow, almost weary
like a nurse on night-shift coming home
the B-52s loom into the morning;
we feel the chill of their shadowing wings
and guilty relief; the bombracks are empty
the war here still unimagined
where they have been and what they have done.

Earlier I saw two cock pheasants
gaudy as subalterns in full dress uniform
bowing and rearing in ritual combat
with me at dawn the only witness
in another region of the same reality.

DESERTED GARDEN

The people have left suddenly.
Disconsolate, the yard cat
will loiter, expecting to be fed
then go off into the wood to kill
but still return each night in hope
an open door'll admit her to the hearth.

In mustered ranks of light green crinolines
the lettuce shoot; strawberries ripen and succumb
to birds and grubs and rot; bramble and thorn
have overwhelmed the gate while tunnelling invaders
creeping elder and deadly nightshade sprawl
across the patch last year was cleared and dug.

Weather loosens fences, doors of barns
their wormy frames gaping from the stone.
Only the ring-doves roo-cooing in the eaves
are constant and perennial in their love.
Forgotten, unharvested, the underearth potatoes
lie waiting for their wild, Edenic spring.

BACK TO EDEN

When they did get there
it was somewhere quite different.
The grass stood high above their heads
and though it swayed and rustled
it was not with the breeze of their passing
and the sound the wind made
was a sound they had never heard.

They saw the lion with the kid it dandled;
regardless of them, it did not arch
its tawny back to their hands' caress.
The branches that overhung their wandering
were not lightened by the fruit they plucked
pears and plums that left no stickiness
no wetness running on their lips and chins.

A place without winter, where night
was a convention ticked on watches
as perfectly light as day. Like the shadows
they could not throw, they slid
over everything, everything slipped from their grasp.
Seeing no way of life, hand in hand
they went out to time's corruption, light and dark.

FRUIT AND VEG

Heroic gardens, layered into hills –
vines, tomato plants and olive trees;
above are mountaintops, above, the sun
blazing and indifferent.

Unrelenting labour, dawn and dusk
to prune and hoe, to cherish this scarce earth
enriched and friable with carried muck
and dung, dug in over ages.

The grey-black outcrops in the terraces
are peasant backs, successive generations;
rock extrusions, impassive sentinels
erode more slowly.

BAD BREATH

August, heavy with reproach
comes too close, reeks of wine
petrol, the microlife of drains.

I climb out on the roof
seeking clearer air
but it's thick and sick with age
furred with memories:

pictures of Africa
that ricochet from space
travelling round or through me
to land on screen like spit.

I breathe the pictures in
my throat and lungs constrict
I sneeze, my eyes fill up with tears.

EXILE

High above the city of Dhaka
arrowing upwards on her jet plane
she remembers the courtroom, the crowds, the heat
her brother's arm, the old men.

She remembers their stern and leering faces:
she'd dressed demurely to avoid blame
in a white sari and dark headscarf.
When they made her uncover, it was their shame.

A ceiling fan chopped the air
thick past breathing. She had to fly
like a bird scrabbling out from hot hands
wingbeat by wingbeat into the sky.

The courtyards and gardens of the city of Dhaka
are bright with women. She sees them beneath
and on the streets young men prowling
in gleaming shirts, white as their teeth.

Glass seals her bubble of freedom
trapped oxygen supplies her breath;
colour fades on her flight out
west and north along the exile's path.

When she lands darkness has already fallen;
she is met at the airport by important men.
They take her straight to the tv studio;
from now on, she is always 'on'.

TROUBLE BREATHING

She was sick before, in the sixties; but must
have got better or we just stopped thinking
about her.

So I was shocked to see her with the
down-and-outs in the centre of town behind
the lights of the Christmas tree.

Her face was as white as a leper, her hair
like stained piano keys. I heard her cough

then everyone was coughing, even the
people in warm coats buying presents and
cards.

She was found dead on Christmas
morning, there on the street. Who
remembered her beauty?

Hastily, without ceremony or respect, they
buried her deep, entombed her in
concrete and lead.

My window looks out across empty fields
that are frozen and seem clean. But my
chest is tight

the air is heavy and I hear children coughing inside the house all day, all night.

CHRISTMAS 1989

Wrong to say despaired of; the century flames
dangerous as a firework's last surprise
and beautiful; light falls on our faces
from hand-held torches, from all the carried candles.

Good news comes and comes by television
a corner opens from our lighted rooms
to a place of darkness that is full of lights
and every light a name we had forgotten.

A fitful flame that flickers as it flares
but lights a space too huge for irony;
no matter if it all should come to tears
we've seen what's marvellous, beyond our narrowing dreams.

GOOD FRIDAY

Whirled all day with the world to the west
my thoughts turn back to the east
along lines that narrow to an unseen point
where you are, lord, all day.
All day while I drive round in the car
doing such ordinary things;
I heard it by chance on the radio
darkness at the sixth hour.
Is today the day for the maggot
to feast on deaths and wounding
for the gory heart in the secret drawer
torture as art at the back of the shelf
shameful stabs of delicious pain
for the fallen lord who will rise again?
Rehearsal emotions, safely unreal.
This is real.
How long was it dark in the city of Bhopal?
How long did the cloud of darkness
hang over Kurdish Halabja?
Not from their mouths full of dirt
came the doctrine of forgiveness;
we have cushioned ourselves on carrion
the dead are dead and cannot forgive.
Two thousand years and your dying increases;
we know too much in our ordinary lives
lord, to assume your forgiveness.

THORPE PARK, EASTER 1991

The log flume at Thorpe Park is the highest in Britain.

They've sent the children's photographs:
wind-combed hair, mouths like Os
dizzying down to white water.
As someone said: *The world is not
improvable but we must act
as if it were.*

              The room's corner
open like a sore
is weeping flies
that pattern covers, blacken the piano.
We flick the *off* but people-littered hills
are retinal images, the hoops and whorls
that decorate the air.

              At Thorpe Park
the air is clear. We're met by men
by persons, grown-ups in Disney suits
cavorting welcome. Ceramic replicas
are sold inside at discount prices.

Ask: *Can a man whose skin's on fire
escape to a world of language
when even his grave's inscribed
in letters he never learnt?*
But he understood his wife
while we can't reach the room

where she lies, wounded and untended
on the marble top of an office cabinet.

We sit outside in a cold wind
with our sandwiches and crisps and carton drinks.
The sun fitful and impermanent as goodness
shines now here, now over there
leaving us in shadow.

        Five o'clock:
our tacky thrills are ended; the crowds
stream by, but they are not undone.
Tired children are carried out to cars
and safely home.

INTERNED

She is held, her life is on hold;
her eyes glitter out of the darkness
even by day on the parched field
she is wired from the shifts of the sun
and dry season follows rainy season
meaningless as television.

Her pain is her grown children
whose bodies have blossomed anyway;
she avoids their questions, shackles
her third child by his ankle
and lies down curled round her youngest
to sleep when she sleeps.

THE INTEGRITY OF OUR QUARREL

I walk up the hill on my own
to look down on the patchwork of fields
bed we have made and must lie on.

A stone skitters in the road behind me.
I look back, over my shoulder
expecting you in the form of my shadow.

But you are absent, gone with the sun
gone but invisibly here
our argument endlessly spooling.

The skin on my forehead tightens
across the brow of our mountains
furrows in your frown.

The lines you have drawn on my face
are the ones we have made on the map:
we are two names for the same place.

CASTLEDERG

You wanted me to write a poem
about Castlederg, you said.
Castlederg, I thought
well, I don't know about that.

Not much of a place, is it?
pretty dead, one main street
half boarded up, mean, dull
even the name like a funeral.

For you, it was childhood.
You've told me things that happened:
the man who died of a heart attack
beside you on the river bank;

the tinker family in your father's shop
who were turned away, and afterwards
the case of apples polished, gleaming
with a bite out of every one.

I can't imagine or find words
to call up what your home was like:
perhaps the kitchen and a smell of baking
down the steps at the back;

nor what it was to be cast out
sent away for an education.
They only did it for the best.
'The pen,' they said 'is easy carried.'

Easier than a hod or a bag of spuds.
Your father never owned his house or shop
the Protestant landlords refused his bids.
Your mother wanted you out of that.

Where could he go but the bottle.
Your mother endured but the slow stain
of rancour absorbed her, grief and illness.
The funerals began.

There was nothing to go back for
but you went back and back and back.
Seven years later you trailed me with you
through the dank ruins of a small town.

There was your grandmother in the shop
where everything had crept up to its sell-by date.
'Is that the Protestant?' she hissed
'Come you with me.' I waited.

Later she was always perfectly mannered.
They're all dead now, your father, your aunt
your granny lived longest, so saw most
of that dreary, unpermitted despair.

The grocery business became a shoe shop
owned by a Protestant, in the UDR;
it was on tv when they shot him dead
as he came down your stairs, to your door.

PLACE NAMES

In memory of Olive Tait

1

Dedication

We are the ones who hold back
lurking in the corner, our tongues as awkward
as the hands we don't know what to do with.
Our mouths are pebble-stopped and cannot utter
the words that pebble-smooth mean only comfort.
Later, too late, we find whole sentences
of curious felicity that memorialise
ourselves, not those they seem to honour.
Too late, I bring these words as gift to you
and to another, hoping they come in time
to be received, face value, as a gift
a token meaning comfort, meaning love.

2

Once, coming off the Larne boat
we missed the road to Ballyclare
and drove up ever-narrowing roads
into the hills above Ballymena.
We were in total and alien darkness, where shapes
only might be whin and dry stone walls
and any light that came need not be friendly.
At last we found ourselves and came down home.
I came back this time to a daylit house
closed as a midnight border, armed and tense
where all the signs were in a foreign language
and the air reeked of unexplained betrayal.

3

Abracadabra, Donaghadee
was what I said when I was wee.
I never say wee now and rarely make spells
but still I can conjure with magical words.
Ahoghill was an old lady in a city ward
trapped by illness, but clear-voiced as a bird.
The wise woman who charmed our styes and boils
was from Aghagallon, like my father's forebears.
I know what they mean to me, Aughnabrack
(my brother's house), Ahoghill, Aghagallon
but there are other meanings locked inside them
intimate namings I don't understand.

4

The children kept asking as we drove along
the road to Derry, the road to Londonderry:
'Is this a Protestant or a Catholic area?'
The fields were bland and green and didn't answer
but all the same I think they were hiding something
nothing's on the surface over there.
Can I decode a sunny afternoon
with a man in shirt-sleeves walking down a lane?
Signs supplant the words, signs and emblems
and even these are dancing round the dark.
Does that explain your increasing silence
an unwillingness to talk, beyond discomfort?

MANNERS OF SPEAKING

'Not bread, Daddy: bray-ud.
That's how they talk in Straid.'

My nephew schooled his father in the village voice
received pronunciation of the shop and school.
My brother's accent is polite Belfast
overlaid with the rural nuances
of his new role as businessman turned farmer.

My voice too is urban middle-class
though growing up I thought the shapes of air
formed by the dancing tongue behind my teeth
curled, or tip touched to the alveolar ridge
as natural and preordained as breathing.

English is my language, English is my history
an English planted in a stony subsoil
that thrusts up still in place names I can say
but can't translate; and yet that ignorance
has shaped the sound that's given me my shape.

My nephew is centred still in innocence
where human beings speak the same way he does.
I hear in him Ulster saying No
and my voice in England is a broadcast warning
against unattended parcels in a public place.

NIGHT

Safe in the bright ways of daylight
she prefers the road between villages
ingenuous under the sun.

Configurations of houses and fields
and the place she is going are known
sure, and appear as expected.

She's secure in the eye of God
whose power hums in the cable
and forces the green-white shoots
through earth to next year's harvest.

But the planet itself cannot bear
such constant unshaded attention
and whirls her through huge distances
as it turns away to the night

where truth is unlit between villages
and the dark can swallow or bruise.
She quails at the absolute strangeness

and with eyes full of borrowed light
will not look out to the cold
and extending ranges of space.

TOWARDS RATHLIN

With all of you in an open boat
up to our ankles in shallow water
I snap off short answers
and skim them over the waves.

Drizzle and a cold wind.
Soaked to the skin, we shrink
from the rain-stiff clothes that encase us
into ourselves, our diminishing warmth.

There are monsters below us, beyond
water, stippled and curtains of water
we can see nothing, only grey
and its intensification in shadows.

Down there and over there
hazards equal in strangeness.
No time to find out: we're sinking
without ever leaving the boat.

CLOUD

For Judi

Like a black udder lowering over us
end of summer clouds shadow the road;
it is the future hanging over us
sky, too often stretched, sags with the load.

Midmorning sun laser zaps the threat
the blue is flat and clean, no scar, no mark;
in summer's playground still, we can forget
autumn, illness, work, the early dark.

One foot connects her to the breathing earth
precariously, as it shifts to another season.
Autumn's change becomes the winter's birth
sharp and keen, bitter wind on skin.

Stripping down to that November air
is each year harder; fear of driving rain
that lashes cheeks, leaves fingers numbed, then sore
pulls down the blinds, insulates the brain.

As it turns, the earth will spin her off
the clouds have opened, her footholds washed away;
her chipped and broken nails cling on to life
with a lacerating grip that slips each day.

That is the window I can't look out of
out there, where wind blows sand against the glass
where, beyond the swirling grit, there is the sight of
people drowning, leaves me speechless.

Where the dark swell, cloud, landmass meet
at the very edge and furthest point of vision:
to be a wedge, an arrow forcing them apart
like watering eyelids, is the one way on.

AT HOME

He will not lift his eyes
beyond two butterflies
dancing their duet above the flowers;
he concentrates his gaze
on the cats that laze
steeped in sun beside the path.

He knows the door is open
and the hall's congested darkness;
he hears the sound of screaming
and knows the words they scream.

They have not seen him yet
waiting at the gate.
The sun is warm against his back
and so he hesitates
before entering through the garden
past butterflies and cats.

HOUSE MOUSE

Like any small brown creature
surviving between stonework and plaster
she depends on being unnoticed
her skill is not to be seen;
you know only the space of her going
the silence as air closes over.

You miss the crumbs from your table
your whiskey levels are lower
and sheet by sheet the ream of laid paper
on the top shelf is diminishing.

But do not call the black cat
nor the man with his vanful of poisons.
Give her houseroom; let her lodge
in the crevice of your not understanding -
rent-free, forget about profit -
and she will leave you inscrutable gifts.

ONLY WORDS

I have too many words in my house:
they pour from mouths on the screen
spill off the shelves in disorder.
I hide in the kitchen for silence
where language is only for labels
but the radio broods in the corner.

At the table with coffee and you
I watch the steam spiral up
separately, from separate cups.
Have I told you I'm thinking of leaving
sneaking out at dusk one evening
unmarked, without letter or note.

Between the brackets of water and grass
I can imagine freedom from speech
like disturbances that ripple the river
unaccountably subtle and various;
or the train that moves through the landscape
recreated moment by moment.

But this is an invisible journey
which stops at a lake of darkness
and the lights that come limping behind
are the words I was running away from.
Like a child who left home between meals
I creep back into the room.

LET THERE BE COMMERCE BETWEEN US

They say now that a healthy heartbeat
is always irregular, a changing pattern
of single events whose fragile rhythm
affirms response to our moments of knowledge.

I could compute the universal sum of heartbeats
but to know them as I knew our unborn children's
their mountains and valleys on the ultrasound screen
and pulsing within, both me and other.

It's hard to acknowledge your presence and share
though I've felt your heart as close as my own
though you set my pace and the climate I live with;
sky-clearer today, changeable as Mercury

who is also Hermes, god of movement
eloquent, tricky, patron of commerce
and under an older aspect, three times the greatest
Hermes Trismegistos, the poets' god.

LOFT DOOR BANGING

Somewhere above my head
no step to reach it by
a door flaps and gapes
dark as an empty eye
the rain falls through.

The wind in scrubby grass
blows, is still, then shifts
twists in indecision
fidgets winter wheat
storm-blue, unripe.

This morning's mirror-bright
so tight and tense an ache
as glass afraid to shiver
spill as splintered silver
down through the dark.

THE ONE AND ONLY

I am Scorpio:
buried so deep inside myself
how could I creep to my own surface
or into another's skin?

I am Scorpio:
there is a world out there
my scaly pincers deal with
and I need not believe in.

I am Scorpio:
arched backwards in reflexive hate
my tail completes its vicious circle
plunges the poison in.

NEW GROWTH

Perhaps it's asking spring to do too much
to brighten up this house.

Next-door's tree has sent its emissaries
little valentines, across the wall.
They prickle on the eye like blood returning
to a numbed limb. Twenty squirrels romp
in the bare acacia branches and plumped-up pigeons
tumble their courtship through over-wintered leaves.

Inside, nothing moves:
hard-bound volumes under shrouds of dust
hold their silence. Out in the stifled garden
crocuses, where I've cleared away the ivy
push through and flower. I struggle with the windows;
the cords are broken and the weights have dropped:

a rush of air tumbles reams of paper
dust-motes glitter in the pallid sunlight.

TRANSMISSIONS

As the apple's passed from mouth to mouth
with squeals and giggles down the line
juice and saliva mingle on our tongues.

The merest stranger standing in the queue
can spread his message with a single sneeze
our bodies get and act on.

Love narrowcasts good news and bad:
special productions of true stories
archived in successive generations.

Even our machines are interactive;
modems link computer terminals
to share and pass on knowledge.
Our walls are full of holes; the television
squat in its corner, like a third eye
winks and waits, bringing in the world.

Like our bodies, like our smart machines
we are permeable, compatible and different;
surely we can talk.

FEEL GOOD

Dusk, and a drizzle begins to fall.
In the meadow the call of the peewit
is heard, but the bird can hardly be seen.
Here, beside me, a black horse crumples
rolls, over, and again, all the way over
gets up, fit in his skin, and then
for no particular reason, or perhaps
triggered by the sting of the rain, starts forwards
stops, buckjumps and squeals. The charge
of his energy reaches the others; together
like dull thunder, they gallop into the murk.
And I, too, for no particular reason,
feel good.

VISIT TO THE FARM MUSEUM

This has been taken care of; they showed me the place
where the wren builds her nest under the pergola
a new one each year just along from the last
so tiny I would never have noticed it.

With that eye for detail they've furnished their museum:
farm tools, a gas mask, a wooden butter churn
and cast-iron nameplates from forgotten machinery
cleaned and repainted, all for love.

Every part of the garden is known and accounted for;
even the gate has a name and a story to go with it.
Before this required measure of attention
to learn and preserve, I quail, faint-hearted.

One shows us photos of the children's grandfathers
outside the schoolhouse, the village Home Guard
but can't tell us what flowers those are in the garden
his brother's province, the naming is shared.

REMEMBRANCE SERVICE
AT WHEATLEY PARK

'Aintcha got a poppy, miss?'
Irresolutely poppyless
I follow the children into the school hall.
Their teachers seat them, row on row
cross-legged on the dusty floor.
Furled standards lean against the wall
while veterans of the second war
straggle in; we find them chairs
and children's voices speak the words
of those whose tongues so long ago
were stopped. They were also young
and came like these from villages
where their names on the war memorials
are the same as on this school's rolls.
A sixthform girl playing the Last Post
is followed by a ragged silence.
The ghostly fabric of a tattered flag
unfolds and wraps them in its remnants.

GRACE

It was there
a black and white rabbit
not a cat or a hare;
black rabbits are not uncommon
albinos (white) are rare
except on some off-shore islands.

Was it a pet?
Will it be caught
by a fox or a cat?

No house is near.
Why then
not even every afternoon
does it appear
at the same place in the lane?

We didn't expect it to come;
how will we know
when it's not coming back?

REDEMPTION SONG

Brought up that way, with fairytales
animals that talked from heads at either end
doors that opened into other worlds
she knew her fact from fiction, but retained
a feel for marvels. She liked to be wide-eyed
so took their word; they called her gullible.

Her brother span her yarns:
told her once the German V-1 rockets
were launched from an Antrim hillside
a place she knew and rode by often
a place where winds blew unhindered
across the backs of black cows
stubbornly chewing the sallow grass
where barbed wire flapped from rusted fenceposts
and crazed concrete cracked in chunks
sank into the sullen earth.

When it came to the hill
she was easy to fool
still half-believed the host lived under it
or ghosts of the past, below layers of time.

After God and religion
she abandoned fairies
but relied on words
as the matter of trust

lazily literal
she forgot ambiguity
and even lies
are approaches to truth

acting as if
people meant what they said
her excuse for amazement
at the way they behaved.

Until the hard men came from out of the hill
not as she imagined, in green and silver;
but men whose faces the earth had eaten
with features fresh-painted for whatever purpose
eyes, eyebrows and smiles newly-designed;
only their clothes, as they moved through her house
reeked of mouldering cardboard and damp.

After that she gave up on words
temporary, relative, merely expedient;
she put food in front of them, murmured politely
said hallo and goodbye as seemed appropriate.
She didn't believe them, didn't believe anything
or else believed everything as shapes shifted and fused.

And then one day a boy wrote a poem
instead of his homework, instead of his classwork
he kept writing poems and when she asked
she had to believe him, he told such lies:

Please miss, the rat got it
Please miss, the cat ate it
Please miss, I left it on the table at home
the one by the door with the chrysanthemum
the dog knocked over the week before last.
He looked in her face with ingenuous eyes
and she had to trust him for the sake of the language
for the sake of the words, for the sake of the poems
for the poems and poets of the years to come.